CONSERVING OUR FRESH WATER

by Carol Inskipp

Smart Apple Media

First published in 2006 by Evans Brothers Limited
2A Portman Mansions, Chiltern Street, London W1U 6NR

Produced for Evans Brothers Limited by White-Thomson Publishing Ltd.
210 High Street, Lewes, East Sussex BN7 2NH

Editorial: Catherine Clarke; Design: Tinstar Design Ltd.; Consultant: Dr. Chris Tydeman;
WWF Reviewers: Patricia Kendell and Cherry Duggan; Picture Research: Amy Sparks

Acknowledgements
Alamy **pp. 8**, **30**; Corbis **pp. 9** (Joe McDonald), **15** (Shamil Zhymatov/Reuters), **16** (Keren Su), **21** (Vince Streano), **22** (Theo Allots), **25** (Michael Busselle), **32** (Keren Su), **33** (Chris Lisle), **34** (Yann Arthus-Bertrand), **36** (Tim Page), **37** (Kamal Kishore/Reuters), **39** (Lance Nelson), **40** (Yann Arthus-Bertrand), **42** (Daniel Aguilar/Reuters), **43** (Daniel Frykholm/Reuters); Digitalvision **p. 18**; The Metropolitan Water District of Southern California **p. 41**; Photolibrary **pp. 5** (top) (OSF), **10** (Martyn Colbeck), **12** (Animals Animals/Earth Scenes), **13** (Index Stock Imagery), **17** (Robert Harding Picture Library), **19** (William Gray), **23** (Manfred Pfefferle), **24** (David Tipling), **26** (OSF), **27** (Robin Smith), **29** (Index Stock Imagery), **31** (The Travel Library Limited), **35** (Index Stock Imagery), **44** (Foodpix), **45** (James H. Robinson); Topfoto **pp. 5** (bottom) (Roger Viola), **6** (The Image Works), **7** (The Image Works), **28**.

Cover photograph reproduced with permission of OSF/Photolibrary/Niall Benvie.

World Wildlife Fund-UK Registered Charity No. 1081247. A company limited by guarantee number 4016725.
Panda symbol © 1986 WWF. ® WWF Registered trademark.
Published in the United States by Smart Apple Media
2140 Howard Drive West, North Mankato, Minnesota 56003

Library of Congress Cataloging-in-Publication Data

Inskipp, Carol, 1948-
Conserving our fresh water / by Carol Inskipp.
p. cm. — (Sustainable futures)
Includes index.
ISBN-13: 978-1-58340-977-0
1. Water conservation—Juvenile literature. 2. Fresh Water—Juvenile literature. I. Title. II. Series.

TD388.I57 2006
333.91'16—dc22   2005057616

9 8 7 6 5 4 3 2 1

Contents

A sustainable future for fresh water

Fresh water is water with less than .5 parts per 1,000 dissolved salts. It does not include seawater. Fresh water is a precious resource in our environment. Today, Earth has the same amount of water as when the planet was formed. This means that the water you drink today may have been a drink for a dinosaur. Earth will not get any more water. We depend on the fresh water from lakes, rivers, and groundwater for our drinking water. We also need clean water to irrigate crops, to sustain fisheries, and as habitats for freshwater plant and animal life. The health of fresh water is vitally important for all living things. Freshwater wetland habitats (e.g. lakes, marshes, rivers, and streams) are some of the most important natural ecosystems that sustain life on Earth.

What is a sustainable future for fresh water?

A sustainable future is a lasting one. This means that to ensure a sustainable future for fresh water, we must not take more water than Earth can provide, and we must be careful to protect the quality of the world's fresh water in the long term.

Availability of fresh water

Only around .01 percent of the world's water is easily available for people to use. Water availability and quality are falling, while demand for water is growing at a rate that cannot be sustained. People already use more than half of the world's available fresh water and may use nearly three-quarters by 2025.

Data Source: World Conservation Monitoring Center

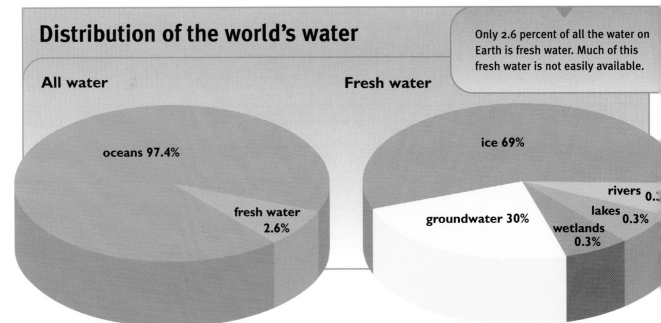

Distribution of the world's water

Only 2.6 percent of all the water on Earth is fresh water. Much of this fresh water is not easily available.

All water

- oceans 97.4%
- fresh water 2.6%

Fresh water

- ice 69%
- groundwater 30%
- rivers 0.;
- lakes 0.3%
- wetlands 0.3%

These African children are collecting water. Africa is the second-driest continent in the world, and millions of Africans still suffer from water shortages throughout the year. Fourteen countries in Africa face problems of water scarcity. Another 11 countries are expected not to have enough water by 2025, at which time nearly half of Africa's population will be short of water.

The amount of water people use worldwide has almost doubled in the last 50 years. A third of the world's population lives in countries that are short of water. By 2025, this is expected to rise to two-thirds.

Water is becoming scarce not only because we are using more water, but also because pollution of water is increasing, and many wetland habitats are being damaged or lost. Safe water is often scarce because it is not valued enough and is used inefficiently. A major problem in many developing nations is the lack of means to deliver water to people, such as wells, pipes, and faucets. Management of water supplies is another important factor. There is much room for improvement in developed, as well as developing, countries. For instance, around a third of London's water supply is lost through leaks in pipes that have not been properly maintained.

Water shortages are often due to problems of geographical distribution. Sometimes there is a great deal of water where there are not many people. For example, in the Congo Basin (right) in Africa, 30 percent of the continent's water drains land that is inhabited by only 10 percent of Africa's population.

Importance of fresh water

Fresh water is one of the most important resources for our well-being, along with the air we breathe. Without fresh water, life could not exist on Earth. Living cells consist of about 75 percent water. While the human body can live for weeks without food, it can survive only a few days without water. People need water for drinking, growing food, washing, producing energy, and for use in industry. Increasing competition for water among these uses is damaging the natural water resources on which we all depend.

Water is essential for life—we all need 5 to 13 gallons (19 to 50 l) of water free from contaminants every day. However, people in developed countries often use far more than this. For example, an average American—who lives in one of the richest countries—uses 105 gallons (400 l) a day for domestic needs, while an average Ethiopian—who lives in one of the world's poorest countries—uses 8 gallons (30 l) a day.

Access to safe, clean water and sanitation are widely recognized as basic human needs. Without safe water, people cannot lead healthy, productive lives. Most people who suffer from unsafe water and poor sanitation live in less developed countries. Those most at risk are children and the elderly because they often have less resistance to disease, so they are more likely to become ill.

Sanitation

Good sanitation means maintaining clean, hygienic conditions and removing human waste, or sewage, in order to prevent disease. In the developed world, sanitation is generally good. However, sanitation conditions are often poor in many developing countries—especially in cities. The rapid growth of cities makes this problem worse. In cities in developing countries, around 90 percent of wastewater runs into

rivers without being treated. Many people, especially the poor, must live among unhealthy open ditches of sewage. Untreated sewage can pollute water sources close to cities, forcing people to pipe water from farther and farther away.

Improvements in water and sanitation lead to better health. For example, improved sanitation in developing countries was found to cut the number of diarrhea cases by a quarter to a third.

Nearly half of the people in the developing world suffer from diseases, such as cholera and diarrhea, caused by lack of safe water and sanitation. Many of these people must rely on feeding stations, such as this one in Somalia, for safe water and food.

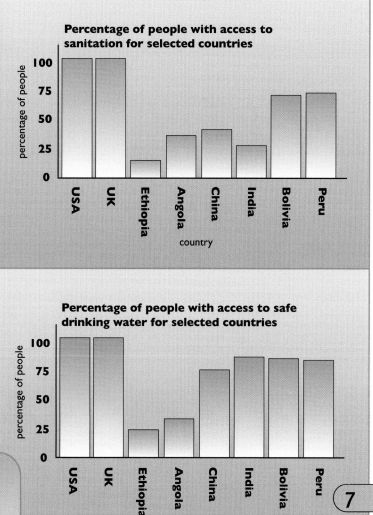

Many people in developed countries waste water because it seems to be plentiful or cheap. In contrast, getting water is more difficult and often more expensive for the poorest people in developing nations. In rural areas, women and children may spend up to eight hours a day fetching water from wells such as this one in India.

Data Source: United Nations Development Program Human Development Report, 2004.

Fresh water facts

▶ More than one billion people worldwide do not have enough safe water for their daily needs—that's about one-sixth of all people on Earth.

▶ Two and a half billion people do not have access to improved sanitation.

▶ Five million people, mostly children, die each year from illnesses related to poor-quality water.

▶ According to the World Health Organization, five gallons (19 l) of water are needed to meet one person's daily needs.

▶ At least one in three people living in Asia have no access to safe drinking water, and at least one in two have no access to adequate sanitation.

Data Source: WWF

Almost everyone who lives in a developed country has access to safe drinking water and proper sanitation. In developing countries, however, sometimes less than half the population has access to these things.

Percentage of people with access to sanitation for selected countries

percentage of people: 100, 75, 50, 25, 0

country: USA, UK, Ethiopia, Angola, China, India, Bolivia, Peru

Percentage of people with access to safe drinking water for selected countries

percentage of people: 100, 75, 50, 25, 0

country: USA, UK, Ethiopia, Angola, China, India, Bolivia, Peru

Freshwater ecosystems

Freshwater ecosystems consist of all of the plants and animals in a freshwater habitat, together with their freshwater environment. They can include tiny village ponds, lakes, bogs, marshes, streams, rivers, and desert oases.

Why freshwater ecosystems are valuable

Freshwater ecosystems are often undervalued. Besides giving us water for drinking and cooking, they provide a large range of goods and services that are vital to our quality of life and even to our survival. These goods and services include:

Food and water

Freshwater wetlands are abundant sources of food, including fish, shrimps, and wild birds such as ducks and geese. They provide important sources of protein for many of the world's poor people.

Water needed for irrigating crops can be provided by wetlands. One of the world's most important crops is rice, which forms the main diet of nearly three billion people—half of the world's population. Rice is grown in wetlands across Asia and west Africa and in the United States.

Other products

Reeds from wetlands are used for roofing and provide livelihoods for weavers of mats and baskets. Valuable oils for cooking and soap-making can be extracted from palms growing in African wetlands. Medicinal plants, peat for fuel, and poles for building are all produced in wetlands.

Controlling floods

Floodplains are broad, flat areas of low-lying land near rivers and lakes that are vitally important as natural stores of water and in controlling floods. They act as giant sponges, absorbing rainfall and releasing it over time.

Removing pollutants

Wetlands can absorb chemicals, filter pollutants and sediments, break down pollutants, and neutralize harmful bacteria. In this way, they act like highly efficient sewage plants.

Recycling nutrients

Another important role of freshwater wetlands is the recycling of nutrients, which are chemicals that are essential for the growth of all plant and animal life. These chemicals are recycled over and over again within ecosystems.

Fish from Lake Malawi provide around 70 percent of animal protein eaten in Malawi. Poverty and high population increase in the country have created pressure on the lake's fish stocks. Nearly a quarter of a million people are employed due to the fishing industry, but their jobs are threatened by falling fish populations.

Places for recreation

Wetlands around the world are wonderful places for recreation. Swimming, sailing, canoeing, fishing, and wildlife watching are just some of the activities we can enjoy in lakes and rivers. Visitors and tourists who take part in recreation at wetlands provide valuable income for local communities.

The Economic value of freshwater wetlands

A major study has found that freshwater ecosystems provide more income and wealth to people per unit area than any other type of ecosystem.

Source: WWF International, 2004

Economic value of the Charles River basin wetlands, Massachusetts

The Charles River basin wetlands in Massachusetts consist of one and a third square miles (3.5 sq km) of freshwater marsh and wooded swamp.

The benefits from the wetlands include flood control, recreational values, reduction of pollution, and water supply.

Economic benefit	Money saved or money made per year
Preventing flood damage	$39,986,788
Reduction of pollution	$24,634,150
Recreational/ amenity value	$30,866,063
Total	$95,487,001

The Everglades National Park, Florida, is home to the snowy egret. The Everglades wetland once extended from Lake Okeechobee in the north to Florida Bay in the south. Today, more than half of the original Everglades has been drained. Large quantities of fresh water have been diverted to drain land for agriculture and to allow the building of coastal cities. Wetland habitats in the Everglades are still very important for the region's multibillion dollar tourism and fishing industries. With south Florida's population estimated to double by 2050, the Everglades must be used sustainably to cope with the growing human pressure.

Water and nature

Water moves in a never-ending cycle. Vast quantities of water are continually being recycled through Earth's oceans, land, and atmosphere. This large-scale recycling of water controls our weather, supports plant and animal life on land, and shapes Earth's surface. The water cycle is one of the basic natural systems that makes life on Earth possible.

Mountains—the water towers of the world

Mountains are the world's water towers. They form a barrier to moving air masses that are then forced to rise in order to cross them. As the air rises, it cools to form clouds, and precipitation (rain, snow, or hail) falls. All of the major rivers in the world start in mountains. Mountains also store water in lakes and as groundwater. More than half of the world's population relies on the fresh water that builds up in mountains.

Although mountain areas form a relatively small area of river basins (the entire area drained by a river), they provide the majority of the river water that flows downstream. High mountains store water in solid form as snow and ice.

People worldwide have looked to mountains as sources of water, life, and well-being. Mountains have been, and in some places still are, worshipped as the home of gods who provide rain on which the people depend for crops and survival. In times of drought, for example, the Kikuyu people faced Mount Kenya (below) and asked their god Ngai for rain.

During the summer or dry season, when temperatures rise, water from melting ice and snow flows into the rivers and to the lowlands at a time when precipitation is at its lowest and water demand for irrigation of crops is at its greatest. The flow of water to the lowlands from mountains is vital to the well-being of people around the world.

Mountains are fragile ecosystems. High rainfall, steep slopes, and soils that are easily worn away can result in flooding, soil erosion, and landslides. Fast-flowing rivers can carry large amounts of sediment and deposit them downstream. These sediments can be major pollutants of fresh waters. If untreated, wastes from farming and tourist activities can result in water pollution. If water is removed from mountain rivers, for use in farming or tourism, river flows are reduced. This means that there is less water available downstream for other uses. Careful management of mountain ecosystems and their water resources by people who live in mountain regions is therefore of great importance. As water shortages are becoming more serious, it is vital to ensure that water resources are not polluted or overused.

Forests

Forests are critical to the local water cycle. They slow the runoff water (water draining from the land), lessening the risk of floods. Forests also have an important role in protecting soils from erosion, reducing the amount of sediment that is washed into rivers. In addition, the roots of trees on riverbanks provide valuable breeding habitats for fish, sustaining major fisheries.

The water cycle

When rain falls on land, some of it seeps into the ground and some runs off into streams, rivers, and lakes, and eventually into the oceans. The rest of the water returns to the atmosphere through evaporation. More than 80 percent of evaporation takes place over the oceans. On land, about half of the evaporation occurs on the surface of plants through a process called transpiration. When water vapor is in the atmosphere, it moves upward, cools, and condenses, forming clouds. Water in clouds eventually returns as precipitation, and the water cycle is complete.

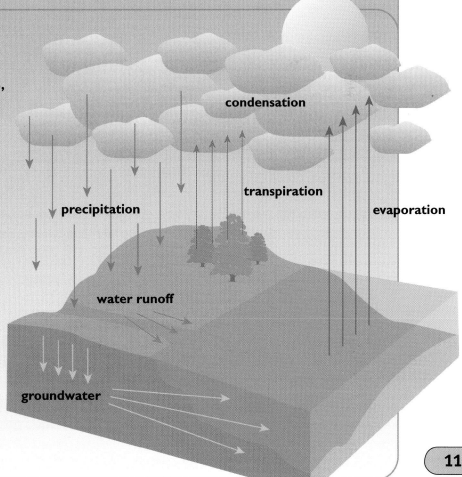

condensation

transpiration

evaporation

precipitation

water runoff

groundwater

Freshwater biodiversity

Biodiversity covers genetic variation, species variation, and ecosystem variation—in other words, the variety of life. Although freshwater ecosystems cover a small proportion of Earth's surface, they support an unusually high number of species. As many as 12 percent of all known species live in freshwater rivers and lakes, although these rivers and lakes represent only .008 percent of the world's water. Around 40 percent of the world's known fish species and 25 percent of all mollusks are freshwater animals.

The Amazon basin is the most biodiverse freshwater ecosystem in the world. This is because of its enormous size—covering 2.3 million square miles (6 million sq km)—and its climate, lying along the equator.

Threats to biodiversity

Freshwater biodiversity is under enormous threat. There are five major causes:

- the withdrawal of too much water from a water body such as a river or lake
- the addition of polluted water to a water habitat
- changing freshwater habitats, for instance by constructing dams or draining wetlands
- overharvesting, usually overfishing
- the introduction of alien species— species that do not occur naturally in a habitat. Alien species may be introduced accidentally or deliberately and can lead to serious declines in native species.

Freshwater fish, such as salmon, are one of the most threatened of all animal groups. In many of the world's largest rivers, freshwater fish stocks have declined by up to 90 percent. Yet, freshwater fish are an important source of animal protein for people around the world and account for as much as 80 percent in parts of South Asia.

Case Study: Water hyacinth—an invasive alien

The water hyacinth is a freshwater plant from the Amazon basin. It is one of the worst weeds in many tropical and subtropical parts of the Americas, Asia, Australia, and Africa, where it is not native. Its beautiful, large, violet flowers led to its introduction as an ornamental plant in some countries. In the Amazon basin, natural enemies, such as insects that eat large amounts of the plant, keep the water hyacinth in check. The annual floods of the Amazon also carry enormous quantities of the plant out to sea.

Water hyacinths on a lagoon in Cote D'Ivoire. In Africa, water hyacinths flourish in every major river and nearly every main freshwater lake. The biodiversity of freshwater habitats is dramatically reduced by the introduction of water hyacinths.

Where it has been introduced, however, the water hyacinth often invades freshwater habitats. It is a very fast-growing plant, and populations are known to double in as little as 12 days.

The plant causes problems because it floats on the water surface and forms a dense mat. This mat keeps sunlight from reaching underwater native plants, so it prevents photosynthesis, the process by which plants produce food and oxygen. The result is that oxygen levels are greatly reduced in the water, and fish and other animal life cannot survive.

Water hyacinths often grow so densely that they can block waterways, stop boat traffic, and make swimming and fishing difficult.

Threats to fresh water

Threats to fresh water are increasing around the world. Too much water is being removed from wetlands for farming, industry, and domestic uses. River waters are being moved from one river basin to another, usually with damaging consequences for the environment. River courses are being substantially altered to help ships travel up and down them more easily. Dam building is reducing the flow of river waters. Pollution is increasing in many rivers, especially in developing countries. Climate change is causing serious changes to the world's water cycle, resulting in floods in some places and droughts in others.

Removing too much water from wetlands

Water is pumped from rivers, lakes, and underground supplies for use in farming and for industrial and domestic purposes. The problem is that very often too much water is removed. The result has often been dried up riverbeds and wetlands and damaged wildlife habitats. Water quality is also reduced, as pollutants become more concentrated in the smaller volume of water that remains.

Transferring water

Huge quantities of water are transferred, or moved, long distances from one river basin to another to help with water shortages. This is known as interbasin water transfer. Many of these projects have been completed since the 1950s, and many more are being prepared around the world.

Unfortunately, transferring water from one river basin to another is not a sustainable answer to water shortages. This is partly because water shortages are often due to unsustainable water management in a river basin. This means that water shortages are likely to continue—even when there is more water.

One serious problem caused by transferring water to another river basin is that removing large quantities of water from a river causes permanent damage to the ecosystem. Another major issue is water wastage. Water evaporation and the seeping away of water from man-made channels often wastes at least half of the water removed from a river basin.

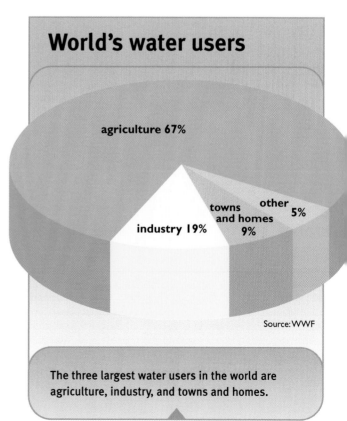

World's water users

agriculture 67%

industry 19%

towns and homes 9%

other 5%

Source: WWF

The three largest water users in the world are agriculture, industry, and towns and homes.

Unsustainable agriculture

Agriculture uses the largest amount of water and wastes 60 percent of the water it uses each year. This is particularly serious for many big food-producing countries, such as the U.S., China, India, Australia, and Spain, which have reached—or are close to reaching—their maximum ability to manage their existing water resources.

Major causes of unsustainable agriculture are poor water management and overuse of pesticides and fertilizers. Although water from leaky irrigation systems returns to the water cycle in the long term, it can lead to waterlogging of soils, reduces river water flows, and damages wildlife habitats in the short term. In developed nations, subsidies (government payments made to farmers) are forcing farmers to produce more food and fiber than are needed. Intensive farming practices are also encouraged. These practices use too many farm chemicals that pollute streams and rivers. Governments are giving more importance to short-term profits than to the long-term benefits of protecting the environment.

In the Mediterranean region, the subsidies paid to farmers are encouraging the growth of crops that are unsuitable for the natural conditions there. For instance, growing strawberries in Andulacia—a very hot, water-stressed area in Spain—is using huge amounts of water and has severely damaged freshwater ecosystems in the country.

Just four crops—cotton, rice, sugarcane, and wheat—account for 58 percent of the world's irrigated farmland. Cotton growing has one of the most severe impacts on freshwater ecosystems around the world compared to other crops. Almost three-quarters of the worldwide cotton harvest comes from irrigated land. Overuse of water in farming harms the environment by causing rivers, lakes, and underground water sources to dry up.

Over time, irrigation can cause soil to become salty. This is because almost all water other than natural rainfall contains some dissolved salts. When plants use the water in soil, these salts are left behind and gradually build up, causing the soil to become saline (salty) and making it impossible to continue to grow crops.

Changes to rivers

River courses have often been straightened and deepened to make transportation and navigation easier. Dams have been built to store water and to create hydroelectric power. Of the 230 major rivers in the world, around 60 percent are thought to be seriously affected by dams, dikes (large ditches), and dredging (deepening of existing waterways). These changes prevent the natural flooding of rivers that takes place in most years. Natural flooding is valuable because it restores waters in wetlands and groundwater, and deposits fertile sediments. Physical alterations to rivers, especially dams, reduce the water flowing downstream in rivers. Pollutants entering the rivers remain the same and are more concentrated in a smaller amount of water. This means that freshwater wildlife is at a much greater risk of being poisoned. Where this affects fish, there is also an effect on fishermen's livelihoods. Dikes may cut rivers off from their natural floodplains, resulting in flooding downstream and sometimes causing serious damage in towns and cities.

"This dam is a fantastic feat of engineering. It will benefit two million Chinese people by providing them with cheap electricity. By building the dam, we will also be able to control the water levels in the Yangtze and so prevent flooding, which is a major problem for people living close to the river."

Dam engineer

"All the people in our village were moved from our homes to make way for the Three Gorges Dam. We were farmers and were promised compensation and new land to farm, but so far, we have received little money, no land, and no alternative jobs."

Farmer

The Yangtze in China is the river most at risk from dams, with 46 large dams planned or being built. This includes the Three Gorges Dam (shown below, under construction). The Yangtze basin is rich in biodiversity, with about 322 fish species and 169 species of amphibians. Species at risk from these dams include the Chinese alligator, the most threatened crocodile species in the world, and the Yangtze river dolphin, the most threatened of all the world's dolphins and whales.

The Rhine River is one of the busiest shipping routes in the world. More than one million containers travel up and down it each year. To enable 550 miles (880 km) of the river to be navigated, 450 dams were built, and many river bends were straightened, making the river 25 percent shorter. These changes have resulted in a breakdown of the Rhine's ecosystem. No migratory fish are left, and wetlands and river forests have vanished. During the last 10 years, there have been heavy floods, causing millions of dollars worth of damage. Each year, hundreds of millions of dollars are spent to manage the river better by restoring wetlands.

The Nile River flows through Ethiopia and then Egypt before reaching the sea.

"Ethiopia is one of the world's poorest countries. We desperately need to withdraw water from the Nile River to irrigate our farmland and feed our people. We need the Nile water more than Egypt, which is 10 times richer than we are."

Ethiopian

"Egypt has relied on the water from the Nile River since ancient times to support its agriculture. But nowadays, we are receiving less and less water as Ethiopian farmers are withdrawing too much to irrigate their crops. If this continues, we will not have enough water for our farms, and crops will fail."

Egyptian

Transboundary rivers

Rivers with basins that are shared by at least two countries are called transboundary rivers. There are 261 major transboundary rivers in the world, and their basins cover an area of about two-thirds of the continents and support two-fifths of the world population.

There are few agreements dealing with the management of these shared river basins. Actions taken by one country can have major impacts on countries downstream. For example, dams built in China on the Mekong River are damaging fisheries and wetlands as far south as Cambodia, more than 620 miles (1,000 km) away. If countries upstream choose to divert water for their own use at the expense of countries downstream, it could lead to conflict or even war.

Pollution

Water pollution happens when harmful substances get into water habitats such as lakes and rivers. These substances dissolve in the water, float in the water, or settle on the water's bed. They reduce the quality of the water, and some can reduce the level of dissolved oxygen in the water, which is vital for the survival of most aquatic life. These consequences can be disastrous for freshwater ecosystems. The pollutants may also seep through the ground and contaminate groundwater and even end up in drinking water supplies.

Sources of pollution

Many human activities can pollute water. Industry, farming, domestic sewage, transportation, and abandoned mines can all affect water quality. Pollution comes from either "point sources," such as discharges from pipes, or from scattered sources, often called "diffuse sources." Wastewater from sewage plants and industry is a point source. Diffuse pollutants include nutrients, such as nitrogen and phosphorus from the overuse of fertilizers in farming, and wastewater that runs off roads, parking lots, and industrial estates, picking up pollutants on the way. Sulfur dioxide and nitrogen oxide gases from power stations, industry, and vehicles are other diffuse pollutants because winds and air currents quickly spread them through the atmosphere. Sources of diffuse pollution may be small, but together, their impact can be very damaging.

In recent years, water quality in rivers has improved greatly in many developed countries, such as the U.S. and the United Kingdom (UK), due to a major cleanup of discharges from industry and sewage plants. However, diffuse pollution from agriculture is still a problem. In the U.S., for example, 22 percent of wells in farming areas contain nitrate levels higher than the federal limit. This drainage pipe has been contaminated with pesticides.

Impacts of water pollution

There are six types of water pollutants:

- Biodegradable wastes. This is waste that can be broken down by living things. It includes human and animal waste, food scraps, and other types of organic material. Biodegradable waste causes water pollution by providing nutrients for bacteria that spread diseases. As bacteria multiply, they use up oxygen in the water that is vital to aquatic plants and animals. Only bacteria that do not need oxygen can survive—and they produce foul-smelling and poisonous gases.

- Excess nutrients—mainly nitrogen and phosphorus. These come chiefly from agricultural fertilizers and encourage the growth of large quantities of algae, known as algal blooms, and other water plants. When these plants eventually die and decay, large amounts of oxygen in the water are used up, resulting in the death of almost all of the aquatic life.

- Sediments such as fine soil washed from the land by rainwater. These can clog water pipes in homes, silt up reservoirs, and smother aquatic life, causing great damage to ecosystems. Water in the U.S., for example, is polluted by more than a billion tons (1 billion t) of sediment each year.

- Toxic chemicals. These include pesticides and heavy metals such as lead, as well as chemical wastes such as cleaners, dyes, and paints from homes and industry. They are serious pollutants and can be highly damaging even at very low concentrations. Chemicals can build up in food chains, causing breeding failure, behavioral changes, cancers, physical deformities, and weakened resistance to disease.

- Thermal pollution. Power plants and industries use water for cooling machinery before returning it to rivers. This water is generally warmer than the rivers and can be deadly to freshwater life because it has a reduced amount of oxygen.

- Radioactive waste. Great care must be taken to store radioactive wastes properly and prevent them from polluting fresh waters. Radioactive waste causes cancer in humans and wildlife and remains at harmful levels in the environment for many years before breaking down.

In developing countries such as the Philippines, an estimated 90 percent of wastewater is discharged directly into rivers and streams without being treated first. Asian rivers are the most polluted in the world, with three times as many bacteria from human waste as the world average.

Climate change

Human activities are increasing the concentration of greenhouse gases, especially carbon dioxide, in the atmosphere, causing the world to heat up. The heating process is often called "global warming," and it is leading to climate change. As a result, some parts of the world are becoming warmer or colder. Some are experiencing floods, and others droughts, for the first time. Many places are experiencing more extreme weather, such as storms and hurricanes. About two-thirds of greenhouse gas pollution comes from the carbon dioxide given out when we burn fossil fuels such as coal, gas, and oil.

The greenhouse effect

1. Heat from the sun

2. Sun's hot rays shine through the blanket of gases

3. Some heat escapes back into space

4. Blanket of gases—this is made thicker with increased amounts of greenhouse gases in the atmosphere. This means that the blanket traps more heat, and Earth gets warmer.

Earth has a "blanket" of gases, known as greenhouse gases, that traps heat near the surface that would otherwise escape into space. This blanket of gases acts like a greenhouse and makes Earth a warmer place. Without it, the average world temperature would be more than 54 °F (30 °C) colder than it is now. This greenhouse effect is a natural phenomenon and is vital to life on Earth, but increased levels of greenhouse gases can have a damaging effect.

The water cycle

Climate change will alter the world's water cycle in different ways. It is predicted that warmer temperatures will lead to a more vigorous water cycle, with more severe droughts and floods in some places. Major floods that have only happened every 100 years may now start to occur every 10 or 20 years. Floods can destroy homes and roads, and threaten people's safety, as well as the survival of wildlife. Areas that are already suffering from drought or flooding, especially in developing countries, are particularly at risk from the effects of climate change on the water cycle because the droughts and floods are likely to become worse.

Glaciers and ice fields are huge masses of ice that are formed on land and move very slowly down slopes or outward due to their own weight. They are important because they contain huge quantities of the world's fresh water. During the summer, melting ice from glaciers produces streams and rivers that are valuable water sources.

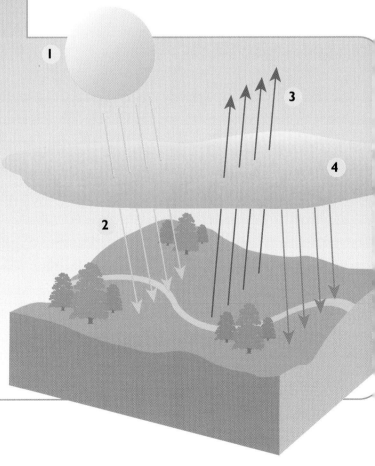

Case Study: El Niño and its effect on the water cycle

El Niño is a local warming of the surface waters of the sea forming an ocean current along the coast of Ecuador and Peru. It normally lasts for only a few weeks each year. Every three to seven years, however, an El Niño develops into a major disruption of the ocean and atmosphere in the tropical Pacific, which has important consequences for the world's climate and water cycle. It may last for many months. The warm-water current carries with it storms that typically hit Australia and parts of the western Pacific. At the present time, scientists do not know what makes an El Niño event happen, although research is taking place to find out. Some scientists believe that global warming is significantly increasing the effects of El Niño.

During the 1982–83 El Niño, one of the worst on record, the U.S. had one of the warmest winters followed by one of the wettest springs ever. Extreme amounts of rain and snow caused massive landslides, floods, and erosion in the West and flooding in the Southeast. Elsewhere in the world, there were droughts in Indonesia, Australia, Mexico, and southeast Africa, while western and central South America had unusually high rainfall. The deaths of more than 1,500 people and $9 billion worth of damage were blamed on the 1982–83 El Niño.

Waves from the El Niño storm of 1983 batter beach houses on Laguna Beach, California. The 1982–83 El Niño caused widespread flooding across the southern U.S. Lakes rose and flooded communities and roads. Landslides destroyed homes and killed people. Rivers flooded and destroyed parts of cities.

Although glaciers have been melting worldwide since around 1850, in recent years, they have been melting at a much faster rate than before. Global warming is melting glaciers in every region of the world. Over the past 50 years, temperatures in the Arctic have risen dramatically. Arctic warming is also affecting Greenland, the site of 10 percent of Earth's frozen water. Every four months, the amount of water that melts from the world's glaciers and eventually flows to the sea is the same as that used by all U.S. homes, factories, and farms.

In Ecuador, Peru, and Bolivia, glaciers supply year-round water and are often the only source of water for major cities during the dry season.

At first, the rapid melting of glaciers increases the volume of water in rivers, bringing the risk of widespread flooding. But in a few decades, the water flows in rivers will decline, leading to water shortages, less energy being produced by hydroelectric power, and less water being available for irrigating crops.

Global action for fresh water

Fresh water is vital to life on Earth, but its future is far from secure. As water demand increases, it is becoming ever more urgent for us to use water resources sustainably. Science tells us that there is enough fresh water in the world to meet present needs and growing populations in the future. The challenge is to protect the sources of fresh water and manage their use sustainably.

Fresh water and sustainable development

If freshwater ecosystems are managed wisely and with care, they will thrive. Communities that live in and understand these ecosystems have a very important role to play. Over generations, many communities have traditionally established codes and beliefs that have balanced and preserved their natural resources. They often have a good knowledge of their surroundings and also of freshwater wildlife. However, traditional ways of life are changing, and this knowledge is often lost.

Governments can also make a major contribution. They can give funds and introduce laws for sustainable development and conservation of wetlands. They can also provide training opportunities for managers and scientists who maintain wetlands. If a wetland is threatened—for instance, by pollution, industrial development, or drainage for farming—then governments can enforce development controls.

Bolivia, Brazil, and Paraguay share the Pantanal, the largest wetland in the world, which covers 53,000 square miles (138,000 sq km) in the center of South America. The Pantanal is one of the planet's most spectacular wetlands and has the greatest concentration of animal life in the Americas. Governments of the three countries must work together to ensure the sustainability of the Pantanal.

Keoladeo National Park in India is an internationally famous wetland that is important for huge numbers of breeding and migratory birds. It is also home to large deer, called sambar (above). Today, the park is suffering from poor management and is under threat from water shortages, overgrazing, and pesticide poisoning. The Indian government has stated that it is tackling the problems, and it is hoped that Keoladeo can reach its full glory again as one of the most amazing wetlands in Asia.

Where freshwater ecosystems cross international borders, cooperation between governments, including the free exchange of information, is vital if these wetlands are to thrive.

If all of this is to happen, governments and politicians have to be convinced of the great value of fresh waters. They need to learn the all-important lesson that to damage or destroy freshwater ecosystems is more costly than managing them sustainably.

World Wildlife Fund (WWF) is one of the organizations calling for the protection and sustainable management of 618 million acres (250 million ha) of freshwater wetlands by 2010. This is more than three times the area of freshwater wetlands that are protected at the present time worldwide. WWF is also promoting activities to restore natural functions to at least 50 large river basins that are vital to people and wildlife.

Ramsar Convention on wetlands

The Ramsar Convention is an international treaty that provides a framework for the conservation and wise use of wetlands and their resources. By 2005, 145 countries had agreed to the Convention. The 1,435 sites, covering nine and a half percent of the world's wetlands—and an area larger than France, Germany, and Switzerland combined—have been designated as Ramsar Wetlands of International Importance.

The Convention has helped to protect wetlands. For example, following the Ramsar Convention's advisory visit to South Africa in 1992, a mining project at the Greater Lucia Ramsar Site was stopped. The South African Government undertook a program to encourage environmental tourism to the area instead. Another key achievement of the Convention has been to raise awareness of the importance of wetlands.

The Convention is facing challenges, too. It can only be effective if its obligations are taken seriously by its member countries. Recently, there has been an alarming increase in the number of Ramsar sites that have been seriously damaged. Examples include the deliberate removal of part of a site in Germany for an airport runway extension and damage to another in Georgia to make way for an oil terminal (a place where oil is delivered by pipeline or tanker).

Millennium Development Goals

The United Nations (UN) is an international organization comprising most nations in the world, set up in 1945 to promote peace, security, and economic development. In 2000, member states of the UN attended the Millennium Summit, an international meeting. The countries agreed on goals for achieving peace, security, and human rights. They also set goals for sustainable development—development that meets the needs of the present, without affecting the ability of future generations to meet their own needs. Their goals included removing extreme poverty and hunger entirely; combating HIV/AIDS, malaria, and other diseases; and ensuring a sustainable future for the environment. One of the goals was to reduce by half the proportion of people without access to safe drinking water by 2015. This means providing access to an improved water supply for 1.5 billion people by 2015— that is 100 million people each year.

World Summit on Sustainable Development

In 2002, the UN held a World Summit on Sustainable Development (WSSD) in Johannesburg, South Africa. The goal was to improve the world commitment to achieving sustainable development. In addition to the target on access to safe drinking water agreed on at the Millennium Summit, nations at the WSSD agreed on a new target to halve the proportion of people who do not have access to basic sanitation by 2015. This means providing access to better sanitation for 1.9 billion people by 2015—that is 125 million people each year. In order to achieve these ambitious targets, a plan of action was drawn up. As a result of the World Summit for Sustainable Development, there are now a growing number of initiatives for improving access to water and sanitation. These include the Water and Sanitation for the Urban Poor project, which works to improve water services for poor people living in towns and cities.

Villagers in Bharatpur, India, may not have water from a faucet, but the important thing is to ensure that the water is safe to drink.

Water for life

The UN has announced 10 years of action for water from 2005 to 2015. The main goal is to encourage efforts to achieve international commitments made on fresh water by 2015. These include the Millennium Development Goals and those made at the World Summit on Sustainable Development. A major effort over 10 years is needed to meet these commitments.

In 2005, five years after agreeing on the Millennium Development Goals, the UN reviewed progress and found that only southern Asia, which includes India and Bangladesh, was on track to halve the proportion of people without access to safe drinking water in rural areas. Progress on sanitation was also poor. While northern Africa and parts of Asia had either met or were on track to halve the proportion of people without sanitation in urban areas, the rest of the developing world was not. For example, in African countries south of the Sahara, only 55 percent of the urban population had access to improved sanitation.

World Commission on Dams

In 1998, the World Commission on Dams was set up to look at how effective large dams are worldwide, to consider alternatives to dams, and to develop practical guidelines for decisions on future dams. The Commission represented all stakeholders involved in the debate on dams, including industry, governments, water resources managers, and people living in areas affected by dams. The Commission found that there were too many

dams where an unacceptable and often unnecessary social and environmental price had been paid. In Mozambique, for example, the Cahora Bassa dam produces enough electricity to supply the needs of all of Mozambique. However, 95 percent of Mozambicans still have no access to electricity. Instead, most of the power generated by Cahora Bassa is exported to South Africa.

The World Commission on Dams drew up a set of recommendations to improve decisions made on dams. The Commission called for all options to be carefully considered before deciding to go ahead with a new dam. This had not happened in the past. The Commission also recommended that problems created by existing dams should be tackled as soon as possible. The Commission made a detailed study and consulted with all those involved with dams. However, its recommendations are still not being put into action in most countries because the Commission has no authority to enforce its recommendations.

The Kariba Dam on the Zambezi River in Africa is one of Africa's largest dams. It produces a huge amount of electricity through hydroelectric power. A few miles away, the tens of thousands of people forced to make way for the dam in the 1950s still have no electricity or adequate water supply. Attempts to eliminate the poverty of these people are now finally being made.

Managing river systems wisely

The best way to conserve the world's freshwater resources is through managing river basins sustainably. In order to achieve this, the management of water within river basins needs to be coordinated with the management of land and other resources. This is known as integrated water resources management.

Integrated water resources management

The economic and social benefits from water resources in river basins should be shared fairly. Wise choices will need to be made about long-term resource use in river basins to ensure sustainable management. Freshwater ecosystems should be protected and maintained because these are the sources of fresh water.

If integrated water resources management is to work successfully, then all stakeholders need to agree on a long-term vision for the future of the river basin. The stakeholders must be well-informed about the interests of all those working and living in the river basin. Stakeholders also need to be actively involved in planning and decision making. Unfortunately, decision-makers, such as politicians, land-use planners, and water engineers, rarely consider river basins as a whole. This is mainly because it is easier to look at aspects of the river basin, such as water, ecology, and social and economic impact, individually.

The need to conserve and manage river basins as a whole is increasingly being recognized. The principle of integrated river basin management is now included in many international agreements. However, turning these agreements into actions means long, and often difficult, discussions among nations to achieve success.

The floodplain of the Kinabatangan River, Malaysia, contains one of the few surviving freshwater swamp forests in Southeast Asia. These evergreen tropical forests are of worldwide importance for their wildlife, including Asian elephants and orangutans. At present, the Kinabatangan swamp forests are highly threatened by deforestation to make way for palm oil plantations.

The Murray and Darling rivers meet in Victoria, Australia. The Murray-Darling river basin has one of the best-developed integrated management plans of any river basin in the world. The plan is having success because it has used the knowledge of local people and appreciates the historical and cultural importance of the river.

"Demand for palm oil is growing, and we need more land for plantations. The Kinabatangan forests must be cleared to make room for oil palms for the sake of our country's economy."

Oil palm plantation owner

"It is of the greatest importance that we conserve the Kinabatangan swamp forests for many threatened species, such as the orangutan and Asian elephant. Without large areas of protected forest, these animals will have no chance of survival."

Wildlife conservationist

Case Study: The Murray-Darling river basin, Australia

The Murray-Darling river basin in Australia spans five states, which makes integrated planning a real challenge. In 2001, the Murray-Darling Basin Commission agreed to achieve a healthy Murray River system that sustains communities of people who live in the river basin. The commission's goals include restoring the natural level of water flowing in the river in places where this is needed and maintaining sufficient water in the river to enable fish to migrate. Keeping the estuary healthy and managing nutrient levels to prevent too much algal growth are other important goals.

The commission discovered it was very important to consult with communities in the river basin. For example, over an 18-month period, the commission actively involved some river communities in its plans. A survey found that 95 percent of these stakeholders supported the commission's idea of returning more water to the river to help the environment. In communities where people had not been directly consulted by the commission about its plans, however, support was less than 40 percent.

Horicon Marsh, Wisconsin. To the west, the Mississippi River contains valuable habitats for fish and other wildlife. The Mississippi has the largest and longest continuous system of wetlands in the U.S. These wetlands provide vitally important areas for large volumes of water to be stored in times of flood. The water is then slowly and safely released into the river and groundwater.

Living on floodplains

For thousands of years, people have chosen to live on floodplains, attracted by the fertile land, a plentiful supply of water, and transportation links provided by the river. However, as these settlements have grown larger, areas of natural floodplains have been built on, and properties in these areas have become increasingly at risk from floods.

The historic solution to such problems was to deepen the river and build flood banks or walls to contain the flow of water. While such measures may keep the people and properties behind the protected area dry, those downstream of the new flood defense frequently suffer. By removing the natural storage provided by the floodplain, more water is contained within the river channel. This causes higher water levels and faster river flows, often resulting in flooding downstream.

Sustainable flood management

A much better and more sustainable approach to reducing the flood risk is to use the natural features of a river, such as its natural floodplain, to manage flooding. Sustainable flood management takes place over the whole river basin. The value of natural floodplains and wetlands is recognized, and these are restored where possible. Construction of new buildings on floodplains is strictly controlled and limited. Buildings that are already in areas at high risk from flooding are removed.

Sustainable flood management involves everyone who manages land in the river basin. Individual agreements often need to be made with land managers. Sustainable flood management can therefore take longer to achieve than building hard defenses such as flood walls, but it lasts much longer and is likely to be cheaper.

Case Study: The Mississippi River basin

The Mississippi River basin is the fourth-largest in the world and covers 41 percent of the U.S. and parts of two Canadian provinces. Large areas of the basin are at risk of flooding, the largest being 35,000 square miles (90,650 sq km) in the lower river valley. Many cities are built along the Mississippi's banks, and all or parts of these are located on the floodplain. For more than 200 years, flood walls were built and river banks raised in attempts to protect land from flooding. Between 1849 and 2005, there have been five disastrous floods. The 2005 flooding was caused by Hurricane Katrina and was the largest natural disaster in the U.S. The floods killed around 1,000 people and resulted in major destruction in New Orleans after the river's flood walls failed.

Since 1969, funds have been made available to people living on the floodplain to encourage them to move their homes and activities elsewhere. However, only 20 to 30 percent of those people have made use of the funds and moved away.

Following the 1993 flood, the federal government increased its support of relocation activities. As a result, more than 13,000 homes have been relocated or removed. Several hundred thousand acres of land formerly used for farming are now being allowed to flood naturally and act as storage areas for floodwaters. These measures have helped reduce flood damage. However, annual flood losses in the U.S. as a whole continue to increase and are currently around $6 billion. Flood losses have increased because, until recently, there have not been detailed management plans to tackle flooding. Efforts are now being made to produce these plans in the Mississippi and other river basins.

Aerial view of the Mississippi River, La Crosse, Wisconsin. Raising flood banks and walls ever higher to cope with rising water levels is not a sustainable approach to reducing the risk of flooding. Despite these structural defenses, there was a disastrous flood in 1993 that caused 38 deaths, the flooding of 6.4 million acres (2.6 million ha), and damages ranging from $12 billion to $20 billion.

29

River navigation

Rivers worldwide are increasingly threatened by being deepened and straightened so that ships can navigate (travel along) them more easily. However, new ways have been found to make navigation of rivers more sustainable.

To achieve sustainability, any changes currently being made to rivers must not damage the ways in which rivers may be used in the future. Navigation should be just one of the uses of the river and not dominate other uses. The ships should adapt to the river rather than the river adapting to the ships.

The interrelationships between living things and the environment of rivers must not be affected by any changes to rivers. Natural processes, such as erosion and the depositing of sediments, should be allowed to continue. Any changes made to rivers should also ensure that plants and animals, and their habitats, remain and flourish.

It is very important that countries through which a river passes work together to decide on a single river basin management plan for the river.

The River Wyre in Lancashire, Britain, is one example of a river that has been deepened and straightened to allow dredgers such as this one to navigate it.

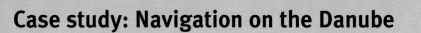

Case study: Navigation on the Danube

As many as 83 million people depend on the Danube for natural resources, and 20 million of them rely directly on the river for drinking water.

The River Danube is one of the most important rivers in the world for inland water transportation. A new European Union program, the Trans-European Networks for Transport, is linking eastern and western European countries. Inland waterways, notably the Danube, are a major part of this plan.

In the past, the Danube has been heavily dredged, dammed, lined with concrete, and straightened. This has resulted in pollution and in huge losses of river and floodplain habitats. Air pollution from water transportation can be worse than from road transportation. Water pollution from ships has created even greater problems. Despite this, the lower stretches of the Danube have remained relatively free from changes, and natural ecosystems remain.

As the new, major European transportation program is developed, a new and sustainable approach to inland navigation is being put into action to ensure the long-term protection of the lower Danube. Technological solutions are being used, such as the redesign of ships with a relatively short depth below the water level (shallow draught) that will not require such frequent and deep dredging of the river. Native vegetation that is part of the river's natural ecosystem is being used, instead of concrete, to stabilize riverbanks. If the river channels need to be changed to allow ships to pass, natural features and habitats of the river and floodplain are being maintained. Pollution controls are also in place.

Shared waters

The natural resources of rivers that cross international boundaries (sometimes called transboundary rivers) must be shared, and shared fairly. Balancing interests is challenging. Some transboundary rivers are managed through international treaties or by river basin organizations that consist of representatives from all of the countries through which the river flows. It is important that countries lying upstream do not take more water than their share; otherwise countries downstream will face water shortages. Navigation rights (the rights for ships to travel along the rivers) need to be maintained for all countries. When one country has plans to develop hydroelectric power, other countries on the river need to be consulted before action is taken. This is because a dam constructed in one country will result in less river water flowing into other countries that are downstream.

Farmers planting rice seedlings in the Mekong River basin. Mekong farmers have been irrigating land for crops for thousands of years. Today, farmers throughout the basin are producing a second, and some a third, rice crop using Mekong River water from 12,500 irrigation systems.

As more countries are becoming aware of the value of using rivers sustainably, they are taking an integrated approach to river management. This means maintaining water levels that are high enough to sustain whole freshwater ecosystems by not removing too much water for irrigation. Closer cooperation between upstream and downstream states is needed to protect against threats to the environment that are frequently caused by dam building and overuse of river water for agriculture, industry, and domestic purposes.

One important step already agreed on is maintaining corridors of land linking important parks and reserves that are habitats of endangered species, such as tigers and Asian elephants. This means the animals can move freely from one site to another.

Case Study: The Mekong River basin

The Mekong River basin is huge, covering an area nearly the size of France and Germany put together. Only the Amazon River basin has a greater diversity of plant and animal life. The Mekong is also a major source of food and livelihoods for 73 million people from 6 countries—Cambodia, China, Laos, Myanmar, Thailand, and Vietnam. Most people living in the basin are farmers and fishermen with very little money. The rich resources of the Mekong's rivers and wetlands make these people's lives possible by providing them with fish and depositing fertile sediments that are valuable for farming.

Economic development of the Mekong is increasing. This is planned along narrow strips of land and water known as economic corridors. These corridors will link major ports and cities with each other as well as with other, less-developed areas. The opening of some of these areas through the construction of buildings, roads, and dams will threaten the Mekong basin's rich natural heritage and the traditional livelihoods of fishermen and farmers living there unless action is taken to prevent this.

At a 2005 meeting, the Mekong River basin countries committed to ensuring that economic development in the basin is environmentally sound and sustainable. The countries agreed on a joint program to help guide sustainable development. This is especially needed in energy, transportation, and tourism, which are key areas of the economy.

The joint program calls on the six countries to investigate and deal with the social and environmental impacts of economic development on the Mekong. It also proposes calculating the values of environmental goods (such as fish and water for irrigation) and services (such as flood protection) provided by the river ecosystem. These should prove the economic value of maintaining a river ecosystem.

Fishing boats on the Mekong Delta. The freshwater fisheries of the Mekong River and its tributaries are estimated to be worth more than $1 billion per year. The people living on and around the Mekong River depend on fish and other food from the river system for most of their protein.

Managing water use wisely

In addition to managing freshwater sources sustainably, we also need to ensure that the use of water is wisely managed. By managing water use, we can reduce the amount of water used and wasted.

Conservation agriculture

There are many ways that water can easily be used more efficiently in agriculture. One of these is to grow crops more suited to the location and season. For example, growing rice requires more water than growing wheat. However, in the Niger River basin, rice is grown in the dry season. Growing wheat instead of rice in that season could reduce water use by more than a third on average, while still producing a crop for food and with commercial value.

Farmers can also reduce water that runs off land and water that evaporates from the soil by using better management. For example, plowing with the contours of the land, rather than across them, creates furrows that are parallel to the slope. Rainwater settles in these furrows instead of running down the slope.

Rows of poplars acting as windbreaks in orchards in Argentina's Neuquen province. Planting trees for shade or as windbreaks can help to conserve water.

Simple new technologies are helping to increase water efficiency. For instance, drip irrigation is the most efficient way of watering crops and gardens. Soil moisture sensors detect when the soil is dry, and then water is slowly dripped at the base of plants with hardly any waste. These can be solar powered and are not expensive.

Much can be done to improve many irrigation systems. Better design, regular maintenance, and effective drainage will all increase efficiency. Where there are water shortages, it is important that water available for irrigation is shared fairly among farmers. Governments can work with farmers and the food industry to develop better management practices. These will increase the efficient use of water and reduce damage to the environment. International environmental organizations, including WWF, are recommending that the European Union, U.S., China, and Japan give money to farmers for better management practices instead of subsidies for growing crops. These practices should include payments for environmental services that farmers provide such as protection of river basins.

Wheat farmers in Jordan. The country is short of water, and only four percent of its land area can be cultivated. Wheat and barley are the main crops. Much of Jordan's food is now imported, especially grains and meat. For example, wheat imports are 10 to 20 times the amount now produced in the country.

Virtual water

We use a lot of water in the production of food such as grains, meat, and dairy products. This water is often consumed without people realizing it, so it is called "virtual water."

A country where water is scarce can choose to import products that require a lot of water for their production, rather than growing them at home. By doing so, the country imports virtual water and allows real water savings. Jordan, for example, saves 80 to 90 percent of its domestic water needs by importing food that requires large amounts of water to produce.

Some countries, however, lose valuable water through virtual water exports. For instance, in the U.S. a third of all the water that is withdrawn from freshwater sources is used to produce food for export. This is a problem in some places, as it has resulted in heavy overuse of precious groundwater.

Rainwater harvesting

Water harvesting is the collection of rain that would otherwise have run into drains, soaked into the ground, or returned to the air through evaporation. By harvesting water, we are not actually taking water out of the water cycle—we are just making more efficient use of water. Rainwater harvesting is a sustainable and relatively cheap form of technology. It is particularly valuable in rural areas where droughts occur frequently or where rain only falls over a short period in the year. For instance, in the Zambezi River basin in southern Africa, more than 65 percent of the rainfall is lost through runoff, yet a number of areas within the basin face severe water shortages. Like many parts of Africa, the water problems of the Zambezi basin are made worse by the short and irregular rainy seasons.

Traditionally, communities worldwide have harvested water for many hundreds of years. One effective method of water harvesting is to collect rainfall from a rooftop and then channel it into a rain barrel, where it is stored for later use. Another widely used system channels rainwater into small gulleys down a slope and then diverts the water onto farmland, where it is used to irrigate crops. In many parts of the world, these ancient systems of rainwater harvesting have become neglected, but in recent years, there has been an enormous revival of traditional practices. New technologies are being used to improve them for modern-day needs in rural areas. Simple technologies such as these for collecting and storing water can help to avoid larger, more damaging storage projects.

Collecting rainwater from a rooftop in Cambodia. This can be an effective method of water harvesting, especially if channeled into a rain barrel and stored for later use.

Rainwater harvesting has great potential in towns and cities that are facing water shortages, such as in India, where most of the rain falls in just 100 hours out of 8,760 hours in a year. It is now practiced on a large scale in some Indian cities such as Bangalore and Delhi. Water is collected from rooftops, and runoff from paved ground is trapped in troughs at street level. Other countries, including the U.S., Japan, and Germany, are also now starting to harvest rainwater in cities. This water is used for a wide range of purposes, and in some places, such as Austin, Texas, this water is used for drinking.

In this village near Madras, India, women use these jars to collect valuable rainwater.

Case study: Laporiya village in Rajasthan

Laporiya village lies on the edge of the Thar Desert in Rajasthan state in northwest India and has rainfall of around 12 inches (30 cm) a year. By the 1970s, the village's traditional water harvesting system had fallen into decay. The villagers were no longer able to continue cattle farming on land around Laporiya. The result was that 40 percent of the people had to move elsewhere to find jobs, and 75 percent of the cattle had to be driven to greener pastures in adjoining states to find enough to eat.

Following a drought in 1977, the villagers started a community project to restore their water harvesting system. They rebuilt broken embankments, repaired storage tanks, and removed silt from community ponds. This restoration proved highly successful and was improved in the 1990s using new, low-cost, very simple, and highly-effective technology. Each pasture is now surrounded by a dike, which stores water when it rains. The pastures are on a slope so that excess rainwater flows into the next pasture until eventually it reaches the village pond, from where the water can be distributed to other pastures.

As a result of the renewed and improved water harvesting system, over the past 20 years water levels in Laporiya's wells have risen by 50 feet (15 m), and crop yields have increased between 3 and 12 times.

Managing the demand for water

In view of the severe water shortages faced by many countries, reducing their demand on existing water resources is extremely important. Countries are classified as water-scarce if they have less than 35,000 cubic feet (1,000 cu m) of renewable water available for each person in a year. In 1990, 20 countries were classified as water-scarce. Another 10 countries will be water-scarce by 2025—assuming their populations increase as the UN predicts. Many of these countries, such as Saudi Arabia and Israel, have hot desert climates. Others are developing nations, especially in Africa—for example, Kenya and Rwanda. Conserving fresh water is very important for developed countries, too. Here, the major problem is that we take fresh water for granted because it is easily available from the faucet. Every drop of water should count. The UN has made March 22 each year "World Water Day."

This gives individuals, groups, organizations, and governments the opportunity to raise awareness of the importance of conserving and managing freshwater sources.

Raising public awareness in both developing and developed nations plays a vital part in ensuring the sustainability of freshwater supplies. The more people know and understand about water scarcity, the more willing they will be to help conserve water.

In about two-thirds of industrialized countries, many homes are now charged for the amount of water used by meter. This can be an effective way of making people use water more efficiently. However, some object to having to pay an additional charge for the volume of water they use, as well as the standard charge for water treatment and delivery to their home.

Water-scarce countries in 1990

Malta	Djibouti	Kuwait	Singapore	Bahrain
Barbados	Cape Verde	Kenya	Saudi Arabia	United Arab Emirates
Malawi	Somalia	Tunisia	Jordan	Qatar
Burundi	Algeria	Rwanda	Yemen	Israel

UN prediction of other countries that will be water-scarce by 2025

Oman	Libya	Morocco	Egypt	Iran
Syria	South Africa	Comoros	Ethiopia	Haiti

Wise and efficient water-use measures are needed. Small attachments that can be screwed on to faucets and showerheads or installed in toilets are very efficient water saving devices (commonly known as WSDs). Even the simple action of turning off the faucet while brushing your teeth is effective in cutting water use.

Flush toilets use as much as two and a half gallons (10 l) of water for each flush. Ultra low-flush toilets can reduce this amount of water considerably. Mexico City had difficulty finding enough water for the city's increasing population, so a water conservation program was launched, replacing 350,000 old toilets with more efficient ones. These replacements saved enough water to supply 250,000 new homes in the city.

Reusing wastewater (water that has been used and is no longer clean) can really help to cut freshwater use. It has been proven to be a sustainable and inexpensive way of creating a reliable and pure supply of water. One common use is for cooling in industrial processes. The Palo Verde Nuclear Generating Station in Arizona uses recycled water for cooling, for example.

Wastewater is valuable around the world in farming and irrigation. For instance, in towns in the West Bekka region in the desert country of Lebanon, wastewater from homes is successfully being used to help the urban poor water home vegetable gardens. Recycled water is also regularly used for toilet flushing, such as in high-rise buildings in California. Nutrients in recycled wastewater can be useful. For example, the water from flushing toilets at Stensund Folk College, Trosa, Sweden, is treated in a greenhouse, where it is used to grow plants and keep fish.

Water recycling has mainly been used for non-drinking purposes up until now. As pressures on water supplies increase and technologies for treating wastewater improve, there are more and more water recycling projects planned that will provide water for drinking. The upper Occoquan Sewage Authority releases recycled water into a stream above a reservoir that provides drinking water in Fairfax County, Virginia, for instance.

Cotton being harvested in Australia. The state of Queensland in Australia has a water recycling plan that encourages water recycling by government, industry, and the community. There is great potential in the use of treated wastewater from towns and cities for irrigation of cotton farming. At the present time, only around 3 percent of treated sewage water is used for irrigation, compared with 60 percent in California.

Desalination as a solution

Desalination is a process that removes salt and other dissolved solids from seawater or brackish water to produce fresh water. In some very dry places, where water is scarce, desalination can be a more sustainable option than using groundwater or surface water, such as rivers and lakes.

There are now more than 7,500 desalination plants in more than 100 countries around the world, with 60 percent of them in the Middle East. One of the two leading methods of desalination is distillation. The water is heated to produce steam. The steam is then condensed to produce water that has a low salt concentration. The other main method of desalination is reverse osmosis. This means that salt water is pushed through a filter that traps salt on one side and allows fresh water to be obtained on the other side of the filter.

Desalination can be an expensive method of obtaining water, although costs are dropping. Another disadvantage is the large amount of energy needed in the distillation method. The disposal of salt produced by desalination can be a problem—for example, if released into the sea, it can damage marine life.

Desalination is carried out in plants such as this one in Doha, Kuwait. In some of the drier parts of the Middle East, where good-quality water is not available or is extremely limited, desalination of seawater has been commonly used to solve the problems of water supply. It provides as much as three-quarters of the total water used by the country of Qatar, for instance.

Desalination in the

In California and other parts of the U.S., small desalination plants have played a part in relieving water shortages. The population of California is growing by 60,000 a year and is putting more pressure on limited water resources. As a result, interest in desalination has increased. As many as 20 desalination plants are in some stage of development along the Californian coast, and others are being considered in Florida and Texas. While some plants are small, others are very large. The proposed San Diego plant would be the biggest in the western hemisphere, producing 60 million gallons (227 million l) of drinking water per day.

If all of the desalination plants that are proposed in California are built, more than a million Californians will be using seawater for their everyday needs. Some Californians are worried that the prospect of plentiful fresh water supplied by desalination would encourage even faster population growth in the state and lead to more environmental damage. This desalination plant is under construction near a beach in southern California.

After years of drought, finding drinking water is a major concern in many parts of Africa and threatens people's survival in some desert regions. Plans for Africa's largest seawater desalination plant were announced in 2005. This will supply 25 percent of the water needed for Algiers, a city where people are desperately short of drinking water. In Botswana, 80 percent of the population depends on groundwater obtained from drilling deep, narrow holes, called boreholes, in the ground. However, drilling for water is expensive and often only results in finding

salty water. Some communities have to depend on water that is delivered by truck, which is costly and often unreliable. Solar power is now being used successfully to desalinate salty groundwater and produce fresh water for isolated communities that live in the Kalahari Desert in Botswana. Using desalinators helps communities to be self-sufficient instead of relying on other people to deliver their water. Salt obtained from this desalination is a useful by-product and can be used for cooking, preserving meat, and curing animal skins.

Providing water services

In the past, governments believed that access to services such as water, healthcare, and education should not be included in trade agreements because these are basic human needs. Today, however, new international trade agreements mean European multinational companies can bid for the right to distribute water in developing countries.

It does not matter who provides the service as long as it is the most efficient and effective, and takes the needs of the poor into account. In some cases, experience shows that selling water on the open market does not meet the needs of poor people who are short of water. For instance, in parts of India where water services have been privatized, some households pay as much as a quarter of their income for water. Throughout industrialized countries, the control of water by private companies instead of government public services has resulted in increased prices, failed promises of improvements, and big profits for the water companies.

Role of the World Bank and Asian Development Bank

The World Bank is a group of three institutions that gives loans to developing countries. It is committed to reaching the Millennium Development Goals in water supply and sanitation. It is heavily involved with national and local governments in advisory work and policy making to help meet these goals. The World Bank has lent countries money for water supplies and sanitation totaling more than $22 billion since 1990. However, the bank also attracts private investors (multinational companies), giving them access to water in developing countries.

When natural disasters such as floods occur in the developing world, the UN often supplies safe drinking water to those affected, such as these Haitians. Even under normal circumstances, it is doubtful that these people could afford to buy bottled water.

What is the real cost of bottled water?

A recent WWF study found that bottled water may be no safer or healthier than tap water in many developed countries, while selling for up to 1,000 times the price. Yet it is the fastest growing drink industry in the world and is estimated to be worth $22 billion per year. Many people buy bottled water because they are worried about the safety of tap water and because brands are often marketed as being drawn from pure sources and as being healthier than tap water. While bottled water is generally safer in areas where tap water may be contaminated, boiling or filtering local water makes it just as safe—and at a much lower cost. While bottled water is often a safer option in developing countries, few people can afford the cost of buying it.

Every year, one and three-quarter million tons (1.5 million t) of plastic are used to bottle water. Toxic chemicals can be released into the environment when bottles are manufactured and when they are thrown away.

The WWF study concluded that bottled water is not a sustainable solution to providing access to healthy water. Good-quality tap water at a fair price for everyone is the answer.

The Asian Development Bank assists in the economic development, and promotes growth and cooperation, in developing member countries. The bank is owned by 47 member countries, which include developing and developed countries in Asia—as well as developed Western countries. Its policies include improving and expanding water services, encouraging the conservation of water, and the integrated management of water services. Like the World Bank, it is encouraging private companies to control water resources in Asia. In this way, both banks are helping multinationals gain ownership over the world's remaining water sources and so are working against the sustainable use of fresh water and the interests of the poor.

Bottled water at a bottling plant in Helsinki, Finland. A quarter of the 23.5 billion gallons (89 billion l) of water bottled worldwide each year are drunk outside their country of origin. This means that significant amounts of the greenhouse gas carbon dioxide are given out in transporting bottled water.

Actions at home

Today, more than ever before, it is vitally important that we protect freshwater resources and use our water supplies sustainably. We can all make a big difference at home, at school, in the garden, shopping, and when we are out and about, even by making small changes to our lives. By saving water where we are, we can help on a global scale—not just have more water ourselves.

Save water by:

- turning off dripping faucets and getting them fixed if necessary—they can waste up to three and a half gallons (13 l) of water a day
- not leaving the faucet running while you brush your teeth
- taking a shower instead of a bath
- using a rain barrel to collect rainwater for the garden
- using a watering can for the garden instead of a hose
- collecting the water used to wash vegetables to water your houseplants
- not buying bottled water if you know your tap water is safe.

Reduce pollution of fresh water

Reduce the amount of waste reaching rivers and lakes by reusing and recycling as much as possible. Cut down your and your family's use of toxic chemicals. You can do this by buying organic fruits and vegetables, not using pesticides in your garden, and using environmentally friendly cleaning products in your home. Encourage your school to do the same.

Never pour car oil or other chemicals, such as garden pesticides, down the drain or on the ground. These toxic substances should be taken to your local waste disposal facility, where they can be disposed of safely.

It is very easy to take fresh water for granted. Next time you have a glass of water, remember that every drop counts!

By e-mailing decision-makers or raising money for conservation organizations, you will be helping to ensure a sustainable future for fresh waters and their wildlife.

Reduce climate change

You can help to reduce climate change and its major impacts on fresh waters by reducing the carbon dioxide you produce. Transportation and energy are the two largest producers of this greenhouse gas.

- Walk, bike, or use public transportation rather than driving whenever possible. If you travel by car, try to carpool.
- Save energy by switching off lights and electrical appliances when not in use.
- Persuade your family to choose energy-efficient lighting and electrical goods.
- Encourage your family to turn down the thermostat on your central heating.

Get involved by:

- joining WWF or another conservation organization; you will receive regular magazines or newsletters letting you know about the charity's work and updates on freshwater conservation
- helping with these organizations' campaigns by sending a letter or e-mailing decision-makers
- raising some money for WWF or other charities working for freshwater conservation
- finding out more about fresh waters and the amazing animals and plants that live there. Keep informed about threats and conservation action by using the Internet and reading books.

Glossary

algae simple, nonflowering plants that are usually aquatic; they are important in fresh waters, as they form the beginning of many food chains, and are also valuable, as they produce oxygen for other living things in the water

brackish describes fresh water mixed with some salt water

climate change process that takes place naturally, but that is being accelerated by human activities, such as the burning of fossil fuels, which interferes with the natural balance of gases in the atmosphere

deforestation the clearing of trees from an area

diffuse pollution pollution that is spread from its source by water or wind

ecosystem all of the plants and animals in an area, along with their environment

embankment a wall or bank of earth built to stop a river from flooding an area

evaporation process by which a liquid changes to a gas

exports goods or services from one country that are sold in another

fertilizer a substance, natural or man-made, that is added to soils to maintain or improve their fertility

fishery a fishing ground or place where fish are caught

floodplain an area flooded naturally by a river

food chain a series of living things that are each dependent on the next as a source of food

fossil fuel a substance, such as coal, oil, or gas, that is formed from the decomposition of animal and plant remains; fossil fuels release carbon dioxide when they are burned

global warming the gradual rise in temperature over all of Earth's surface

greenhouse gas a gas, such as carbon dioxide, that contributes to global warming and climate change

groundwater water from underground sources

habitat the place where a plant or animal lives

heritage valued objects, buildings, or customs that have been passed down in history

hydroelectric power power generated from the energy of falling water in rivers or streams

irrigation supplying water to farmland, usually by a system of canals and pipes

livelihood way of getting things that are needed for life, such as food and shelter; usually livelihoods provide money through a job or the trade of goods and services

migrate to move seasonally, usually over a long distance, from one habitat or climate to another

mollusks animals having a hard shell and a foot, which they use to glide along; oysters and mussels are examples of mollusks

native species a species that occurs naturally in an area

nutrient a food or chemical that provides what is needed for plants or animals to grow

organism an individual animal, plant, or tiny living thing

pollutant a substance that causes pollution

river delta the land at the mouth of a river where it flows into the sea; the land builds outward from sediment carried by the river and is deposited as the river current slows

sediment material that settles to the bottom of a liquid

soil erosion the wearing away of soil and land by water, wind, or ice

species a particular type of living thing

stakeholder anyone with an interest in a particular project or organization

subsidy money given by governments to help an industry or business keep the price of its goods or products low

urban belonging to a town or city

wetlands lands made up of marshes or swamps

Further information

Web sites

WWF International
http://www.panda.org
WWF is an international charity that takes action to protect species and tackle threats to the environment for the benefit of people and nature, and works for sustainable development. WWF runs Adopt a Dolphin and Adopt a Whale programs.

Missouri Botanical Garden
http://mbgnet.mobot.org/fresh/wetlands
Useful and interesting information on wetlands and wetland conservation, both internationally and in the U.S.

Wildfowl and Wetlands Trust
http://www.wwtlearn.org.uk
An attractive site with information and resources on wetlands and their conservation.

National Geographic Wildworld
http://www.nationalgeographic.com/wildworld
Information about the wonders of biodiversity and the urgent need to conserve it.

Environmental Concern Inc.
http://www.wetland.org
A U.S.-based nonprofit organization dedicated to promoting understanding and conserving wetlands.

International Decade for Action: Water for Life 2005–2015
http://www.un.org/waterforlifedecade
Describes actions being taken to meet international commitments to improve the provision of fresh water over the 10 years from 2005 to 2015.

Millennium Ecosystem Assessment
http://www.millenniumassessment.org
A comprehensive assessment of the world's ecosystems, including fresh waters and wetlands.

Books

Graham, Ian. *Water: A Resource Our World Depends On.* Chicago: Heinemann Library, 2005.

Green, Jen. *Saving Water.* Milwaukee, Wis.: Gareth Stevens, 2005.

Morris, Neil. *Rivers & Lakes.* New York: Crabtree, 1998.

Oxlade, Chris. *Down the Drain: Conserving Water.* Chicago: Heinemann Library, 2005.

Parker, Steve. *Pond and River.* New York: Dorling Kindersley, 2005.

Pollard, Michael. *The Rhine.* New York: Benchmark Books, 1998.

Swanson, Peter. *Water, the Drop of Life.* Minnetonka, Minn.: NorthWord Press, 2001.

The Yangtze. New York: Benchmark Books, 1998.

Index